S0-BDR-432

THE
HOME GROOMING
GUIDE FOR
DOGS

THE
HOME GROOMING
GUIDE FOR
DOGS

Adrienne Yorinks

Prince Paperbacks
Crown Publishers, Inc.
New York

Copyright © 1988 by Adrienne Yorinks

All rights reserved.
No part of this book may be reproduced
or transmitted in any form
or by any means,
electronic or mechanical,
including photocopying, recording,
or by any information storage
and retrieval system,
without permission in writing
from the publisher.
A Prince Paperback Book
Published by Crown Publishers, Inc.
225 Park Avenue South, New York,
New York 10003 and represented in Canada by
the Canadian MANDA Group
CROWN, PRINCE PAPERBACKS
and colophons are
trademarks of Crown Publishers, Inc.

Manufactured in the United States of America

Library of Congress Cataloging-in-Publication Data

Yorinks, Adrienne.
The home grooming guide for dogs.

(Prince paperbacks)
1. Dogs—Grooming.   I. Title.
SF427.5.Y67   1988   636.7   0833   87-15521
ISBN 0-517-56773-3 (pbk.)

10 9 8 7 6 5 4 3 2 1

First Edition

For Arthur,
Syd, Bongo, and Selma Kiwi

CONTENTS

FOREWORD

It is a pleasure to have the opportunity to write a few words as a prelude to this good book. Some people may think that a professional book on the proper grooming and coat and skin care of companion animals (I abhor the pejorative term *pet*) is going too far—an example of *petishism* and an overindulgence of pampered pooches. Such is their ignorance.

Regular grooming and attention to the animal's coat and skin is part of the responsible custodianship of our four-legged companions. Indeed, it is one of their *rights,* and the benefits are many.

Social animals in the wild, like the lion and the wolf, as well as most non-human primates groom each other regularly with their tongues, using their teeth (and in the case of monkeys, fingers also) to remove dead skin, tangles of loose fur, external parasites, and potentially injurious burrs and grass seed awns that are difficult for the *groomee* to reach. Biochemical compounds in the saliva also promote healing of wounds and may help cure some skin infections. Furthermore, as I documented in my book on massage therapy, *The Healing Touch,* the social activity of grooming has a bonding function, as between mates, and parents and offspring. And it causes a marked decrease in heart-rate—part of the *relaxation response.*

So it is quite natural for companion animals to enjoy being properly and regularly brushed, combed, and occasionally bathed. It is unnatural, especially for a dog or cat deprived of the companionship of its own kind, never to be groomed by its human companions. This is one of the reasons why two cats or two dogs living in the same house together are often happier and healthier than those that live only with humans.

But regardless of how many animal companions you have, and how much or how little they groom each other, you should groom them every day and not simply pet them when you feel like it. And even by adjunctive massage. Such contact, more so than occasional petting, will evoke the physiologically beneficial relaxation response. This will not only bond your animal companions to you, it is also a wonderful way of communicating and of expressing devotion—a kind of communion if you wish. The beneficial physiological and emotional stimulation grooming provides will also improve the animal's health and immune system because the relaxation response helps rest the over-worked adrenal gland stress-response system. Certainly, many overweight and lethargic cats and dogs are under-stressed. For them a vigorous grooming is a pick-up, and is wisely followed by games, outdoor exercise, and any activity that will arouse the animal to play and explore.

And most of our domesticated cats and dogs need to be groomed—far more than their wild counterparts because they are less healthy—either hyperactive or inactive. This is a result of breeding, temperament, and of how they are raised and related to emotionally by their human companions.

Their environment (especially artificial heat and light) disturbs their natural, seasonal coat-shedding and hair growth cycles and, in some animals, can even affect the pigment of the hair. Thus, many indoor cats and dogs need constant grooming, because they are shedding and growing hair constantly. This could be physically stressful to some animals. It also makes cats prone to gastro-intestinal problems due to fur balls formed from swallowed fur that has been licked out of the coat when the cat grooms itself.

Genetically deformed (e.g., long-backed) animals, and obese, aged, arthritic, and chronically sick ones that cannot groom themselves properly also need special attention and more frequent bathing.

Genetically altered coats, ranging from the long and tangling to the fluffy, never-shedding, always growing varieties, need special attention, and often professional help. Many breeds of dogs and cats could never exist in the wild for long with the kinds of coats that we have given them. This makes our responsibility to care for their coats and grooming needs even greater; it is our moral duty. It is a cruelty of neglect not to properly provide for an animal's grooming requirements, and possibly a punishable offense under most state anti-cruelty laws.

These are some of the many reasons for this book, which is a significant contribution to the proper home care and preventive health-care maintenance for our animal companions. And it is a gift to be shared and enjoyed by all.

Michael W. Fox
Scientific Director of
The Humane Society of the
United States
Washington, D.C.

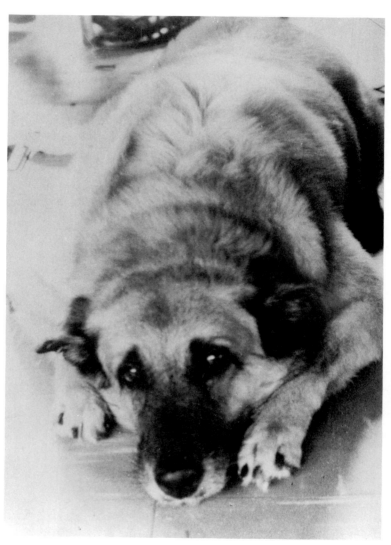

Syd

Juliet Glass

INTRODUCTION

Surely, dogs are our best friends. They are with us through thick and thin, delighting in our attention, attentive to our every mood. When we are happy, they are happy. When we're sad, they stand by us, cheering us up with their warmth and affection. They know so much about us, they seem to read our minds. They care about us with a depth that is hard to find in many of our human relationships. It's rare to find a person who lunges at us with such loving joy as we enter our homes after a hard day at work. Dogs love us and long to please us and ask so little in return.

When I found Syd, a female German shepherd/golden retriever mix at the Animal Rescue League in Boston, my life changed. I was eighteen years old and for the first time in my life I had found a friend so special that I knew right away our friendship would always endure.

Syd taught me a great deal. She taught me how to care and be responsible for another. She taught me that I was special. To her I was the most important person in the world. From the first moment I saw her I felt that we were meant to be together. We suited each other perfectly. We went everywhere together and we had the most wonderful times with each other. I have always loved animals, all kinds of animals, but Syd was my first dog and hence she will always inhabit a singular spot in my heart. Through her wisdom I learned about nature and love and what the phrase "man's best friend" really meant. I believe those early years of caring for Syd greatly influenced my decision to become an animal-care specialist.

In my business, as the Galloping Groomer, I groom dogs and cats in their own homes. With this special service I've had to adjust to dozens of different working conditions, from small studio apartments to palatial penthouses to split-level suburban homes. My canine clients range in age from three months to eighteen years, and vary in weight from four to one hundred fifty pounds. Over several years of working with veterinarians and, in the past, at various grooming shops, I've developed a personal philosophy about grooming that boils down to two overall points:

1. Grooming is a major aspect of preventive health care.

2. Grooming can be a fun and pleasurable experience for both dog and owner.

Consistent grooming is an important key to your dog's living a long, happy, and healthy life. *The Home Grooming Guide* can help anyone maintain a happy and healthy companion animal.

Professional grooming, by a trained specialist, has always been important to maintain the various standard styles of a particular breed. There are many breeds of dogs that require periodic skillful clipping and scissoring to assure a certain look and cut. Poodles, terriers, and long-haired breeds such as Lhasa apsos and Shih Tzus are a few common examples. All dogs, though perhaps some more than others (even mixed breeds), need grooming care.

A dog's hair, if left uncared for, tends to become knotted. These knots are called *mats*. They are very difficult to untangle and can be terribly uncomfortable for the dog. Usually, when faced with mats, the only alternative a groomer has is to strip down the dog. Stripping is removing, by clipping, the dog's coat. As the hair grows back, brushing is required to prevent mats from returning. Before you decide on the kind of dog to get, one aspect to consider is what grooming care is necessary both at home and with a professional. Once you've chosen your dog, deciding the best look for him is fun. Consult your groomer, as well as other owners of the same breed, for ideas. In the case of mixed breeds, whatever seems most comfortable for the dog is usually best.

Home grooming is not always a substitute for a visit to a professional, but aspects of my professional home-grooming care have been adapted in this guide and can be easily used by anyone as a valuable experience for you and your dog.

The idea that grooming can be fun for your dog seems, perhaps, an unusual one, for the image that may come to mind is that of a panicked, quivering, frightened animal trying to run in the opposite direction of the grooming shop or tub at home. It doesn't have to be like that.

When I first took Syd into my home, I, too, held on to the popular notion that dogs hated anything to do with baths and cleanliness. I assumed that dogs, especially big dogs, enjoyed being dirty. But I soon came to learn one of my most valuable lessons: Dogs feel better after a bath! After giving Syd a bath, I could see dramatic differences in her personality. When she was freshly bathed, she pranced around as if to say, "Hey, look at me!" She looked terrific and felt great. As she grew older, she would seem a little more like her puppy self after a bath.

As the Galloping Groomer, I've seen wonderful changes in dogs after they have been groomed. I sometimes walk into a home and see a neglected, surly dog covered with mats. But when I'm done I see a friendly, sweet, and attractive dog. Under the most matted and dirty dog, there is always a dog yearning to be clean and feel good.

As my attitude about grooming began to change, Syd's attitude changed also. I learned another important lesson: Dogs can enjoy a bath! We all have images of our dogs running away as soon as the bathwater is drawn. But what I realized was that as I began to feel that I was doing something wonderful for Syd, she began to enjoy being bathed. Not only did she enjoy the results of a bath, she loved the attention I gave her during it. When I treated the bath as a positive event, a gift of caring and love and fun, Syd no longer dreaded baths.

Many people have negative associations with bathing a dog. I have, on occasion, walked into a home to groom a dog for the first time and heard the owner exclaim in a disgruntled voice, "Uh-oh. It's bath time." At that point the dog is already cowering in the corner.

Dogs attune themselves to our attitude and tone of voice. When it's time for the bath, I cheerfully announce how terrific the bath will be. I explain to the owner that his or her dog should associate positive and special feelings with his bath. Bathing and grooming can be thought of as a session at the "spa," a delicious treat, a chance to be pampered by his favorite person. Dogs learn from our attitudes and they are extremely sensitive to our fears and anxieties. When we are happy and relaxed, they accept whatever we are doing in a happy and relaxed manner.

I am not saying that every facet of grooming is loved by every dog, yet I've never met a dog who hates the entire experience. In some cases, as with older dogs or dogs who have never been groomed, it is more difficult to impart a good experience. But there are always elements of grooming that any dog likes. Syd, for example, loved having her back scrubbed, her face gently washed with a washcloth, and shaking off. I have never seen a dog who doesn't enjoy shaking off after his bath. (Shaking off is when a dog vigorously shakes his body to rid himself of excess water after getting out of the tub or after swimming.)

Every dog delights in different parts of the grooming experience, and these are the moments when you can partake in his excitement and happy feelings. It is important to let your dog fully enjoy the parts of grooming that he likes, and calmly, with extra care, get him through the parts he is not crazy about at first.

Grooming is vital in maintaining a healthy animal, especially since dogs cannot bathe themselves. It is up to us to help our dogs feel and look their best. Dogs who remain matted and dirty for a very long time tend to develop serious and painful skin problems. Once this happens, the owner is forced to take the dog to the veterinarian for treatment. Home grooming is terrific preventive health care. It is an excellent opportunity to check on an animal's overall condition, as well as to notice any changes in the teeth, hair, ears, nails, and pads of the feet. Through caring and consistent grooming we are able to maintain the beauty, health, and quality of our friend's life throughout all of its stages.

What follows is an example of the importance of home grooming.

Dogs' ears are quite susceptible to infection and it is therefore necessary for them to be kept clean at all times. By using my methods, you can take care of this common canine health problem at home.

When I first met Dyoji, an Akita, she would snap at me whenever I would try to clean her ears. Her ears needed to be cleaned, but I didn't force the issue. I worked with her very slowly at first. I never yelled at her. Instead, I tried to understand her discomfort.

Each time I groomed her I took a small step toward cleaning her ears. Sometimes I would speak softly to her as I simply massaged the base of her ear. Other times I would give her a bit of a liver treat as I inspected her ear. Soon, I was able to clean the inside of her ears briefly with a cotton ball saturated with alcohol and hydrogen peroxide. A few months later I was able to clean her ears fairly well, keeping liver treats as part of the ritual and always massaging the base of each ear when I was finished. Eight months later, ear cleaning became one of Dyoji's favorite experiences. She moans with delight now when I clean her ears. Her initial fear and snapping has totally disappeared.

There are many reasons why an animal may act negatively to a certain part of grooming, and it is always important to ask your veterinarian if you suspect something specific is bothering your dog. Dyoji's owner told me that as a young puppy her ears were glued for a long time and that she had had a recurring ear infection which lasted until she was about four months old. (Her ears were glued to achieve the upright look of an Akita's ears, a procedure sometimes recommended by breeders.)

Dogs are sensitive to pain and can remember an unpleasant feeling for a long time. It is important to remember this when you groom your dog and to be very sensitive to his feelings. Dogs respond favorably to our genuine concern toward them as long as we are consistent and clear about what we are doing. If your dog is prone to ear infections, you can help him avoid them by frequent ear inspections and cleanings, which can also be pleasurable for the dog.

I encourage people to learn as much about their dog as

possible. The more you know about your animal, the better your insight will be into his health and well-being. Grooming, and the awareness of your dog that it brings, creates a link between you and your veterinarian. Dogs cannot verbalize their discomfort. They try to tell us in other ways, but sometimes their means are subtle and not easily apparent. Your awareness is the key to an early detection of health problems that might occur. Home grooming gives you the opportunity to be aware of your dog's health on a regular basis.

There is one other side benefit to home grooming which is important to mention. Dogs that are used to being touched are much less afraid when other professionals (such as a veterinarian) or friends touch them. A well socialized dog is more comfortable in strange surroundings and will make others feel more comfortable around him. This, in turn, will result in your dog being welcomed in more places and will also allow you to feel more comfortable about bringing him with you when you visit or travel.

Grooming is a special experience for dogs of all ages. Though it is best to introduce grooming to your dog when he is a puppy, it is never too late to start. Whether your dog is fourteen years old or fourteen weeks old, if you bring to the experience a bit of knowledge, the right attitude, and a whole lot of love and care, your dog will return your attention with appreciation and happiness throughout what we'd hope is his long and healthy life.

1 · BEFORE YOU BEGIN

When Is Grooming Appropriate?

It is best to start grooming your dog when he is a puppy. The more he is used to the experience, as an everyday part of his life, the more beneficial, easy, and fun the experience will be for him. He will soon come to enjoy grooming as a very special event.

I like to start the puppy's first bath after he has received all of his puppy shots (excluding rabies) at about three to four months of age. If your dog is older, though, it is still not too late to develop a grooming routine with him. In my work, I have started to groom dogs as old as fifteen years. If you are starting to groom your older dog for the first time, the major thought to keep in mind is to start slowly and gently.

Whether you're dealing with a puppy or an older dog, patience is the key to building a positive attitude about grooming. Never groom when you are feeling tired or rushed. Never try to groom your dog when you are expecting a delivery any minute or friends are about to visit. Try to do it when the house has settled down a bit, even if that means spreading the grooming into several short mini-sessions. Dogs will respond positively to grooming when they are treated calmly and respectfully. They enjoy the one-to-one relationship in grooming, when their favorite friend is devoting time and care only to them.

How often a dog needs to be groomed very much depends upon the individual dog, the breed, the type of home, and the people he lives with. White dogs, for example, will generally need more frequent grooming than darker-colored dogs. As a general rule, dogs should be bathed every four to six weeks in the spring, summer, and fall. During winter I like to cut down bathing for most dogs to every six to ten weeks. In the winter months, short-haired medium and large dogs need the least amount of bathing. Long-haired dogs such as Old English sheepdogs or briards need to be bathed every four to six weeks regardless of the season because dirt tends to clump to their hair and cause matting. Of course, how often you wish to bathe your dog rests ultimately upon your knowledge of your own dog and plain old common sense.

For example, every dog has a unique smell, as does every owner. The way a dog smells is not always an indication that grooming is required. Many of my customers who have never had a dog before are not used to what a dog smells like. Every breed, to some degree, has a certain smell, and within that breed each animal has his own odor. If your dog has a bad odor, it is important to isolate where exactly it is coming from.

First, check around the dog's rear end to see if any excrement has dried in his hair. If this has occurred, gently wipe the area with a warm, wet washcloth. Also check the pads of his feet to see if the dog has stepped in anything. If so, also wash with warm water, although here you may use a little mild soap, which should be rinsed off thoroughly.

If the above areas are not the problem, be sure to check his ears to determine if it is coming from there. If it is, there is a possibility that he has an ear infection. For ear infections, it is always a good idea to see your veterinarian, who can take care of the problem right away.

Where Do I Groom My Dog?

You should groom your dog preferably in the same place each session. Consistency is always important. The space can range from a kitchen table or kitchen counter for a small dog to the bathroom or laundry room for a larger dog. In some cases it is easier to groom your dog on a table, since you can avoid strain on your back by having your dog at hip level rather than having to bend down to him.

Never leave your dog unattended on a high counter or table and always try to keep a gentle but firm hand on him.

Depending on your home or apartment, grooming may require two separate locations, one for brushing and another for bathing and finishing touches. You may want to brush your dog in the living room, where you are relaxed, and bathing, of course, will be done where there is a tub or sink. In the summer you can wash your dog outside, provided you have access to both hot and cold running water. Never use cold water alone to bathe your dog. Not only is it dangerous for his health, but it won't rinse out the shampoo well.

To prepare the area you choose, remove all unnecessary objects to avoid accidents. To protect your kitchen table or countertop from scratches, use a rubber bath mat or pad. This will also keep your dog from slipping or sliding. Keep all the tools and equipment you will need to do the whole job near you so you won't have to leave your dog in the middle of grooming in order to fetch an item. And as for yourself, wear comfortable old clothing, as you're bound to get a little bit wet, at least the first time around.

Let me mention here one word about professional grooming tables. A professional grooming table is fine to use if you have one, but I never use the arm attachment and noose, which is generally the norm in grooming shops. I feel it is a barrier to the enjoyment of grooming. It is uncomfortable for the dog and defeats the purpose of my methods. The control you have over your dog is best accomplished with love and understanding and the belief that what you are doing is in the best interest of your dog's health and well-being. If you can communicate that to your animal with patience, he will learn not only to behave, but also to enjoy being groomed.

What Do I Need for Home Grooming?

Many of the supplies you will need are already in your home. As I said, it is best to have everything set aside before you begin grooming. You might want to put all of the grooming articles in a small box or drawer near the grooming area and keep these reserved for your dog. For example, you can use

Lewis Jackson

Brushing Nanoosh, a bearded collie, on dining room table

small plastic bottles to hold alcohol, hydrogen peroxide, and baking soda so you will always have them available for grooming. Don't forget to label all of your plastic bottles with masking tape.

SUPPLIES

1. Alcohol
2. Hydrogen peroxide
3. Cotton balls
4. Nail clipper for dogs and dog nail file or emery board
5. Cut stop or styptic pencil
6. Baking soda
7. A child's soft toothbrush
8. Brushes
9. Combs
10. Shedding tools
11. Shampoo and creme rinse
12. Detachable shower head with hose (such as a shower massage) or a hose attachment for sink or tub
13. A bath or sink mat
14. Blow-dryer
15. At least two towels
16. Favorite dog treats (used only for grooming)
17. LOTS OF PATIENCE

It is important to ascertain the type of coat your dog has in order to choose the right grooming supplies. The following chart will help you determine which brushes to use.

BREED AND BRUSH CHART

Coat Type (Breed Examples)

	Poodle type (NON-SHEDDING)	Terriers and schnauzers (WIRY COAT)	Long-haired small dogs (SILKY)	Long-haired large dogs (SILKY)	Silky or curly coat with light feathering	Short-haired dogs (LIGHT SHEDDING)	Double-coated dogs (SHEDDING)
Breed examples	Bichon frise, all poodles, Bedlington terrier	Airedale, cairn, wire-haired fox terrier, West Highland terrier. most terriers, and all schnauzers	Maltese, Lhasa apso, Shih Tzu, Yorkshire terrier, silky terrier	Afghan hound, Old English sheepdog, bearded collie	Springer spaniel, Irish setter, golden retriever,* Bernese mountain dog,* King Charles spaniel	Dalmatian, Labrador retriever, Doberman pinscher, pug, Chihuahua	German shepherd, Akita, Siberian husky, Samoyed, collie, chow chow
Care	Brush and comb daily Bathe monthly	Brush daily Bathe every 6–8 weeks, 6–10 weeks in winter	Brush and comb daily Bathe monthly	Brush and comb daily Bathe monthly	Brush and comb twice a week Bathe every 6–8 weeks, 6–10 weeks in winter	Brush weekly Shed out seasonally Bathe every 6–8 weeks, 6–10 weeks in winter	Brush twice a week Shed out seasonally Bathe 6–8 weeks, 6–10 weeks in winter
Tools	Fine wire slicker brush, pin brush, double-sided comb, de-matting comb	Fine wire slicker brush, bristle brush	Pin brush, fine wire slicker brush, small de-matting comb, double-sided comb	Pin brush (large), curved slicker brush, large-toothed comb, large de-matting comb	Pin brush, fine wire slicker brush, double-sided comb	Bristle brush, rubber palm brush, small rake (for cats)	Fine wire slicker brush, pin brush, large rake, under-coat comb

*Sometimes these dogs are considered double-coated . It will depend on your individual dog. If your dog is shedding a great deal, use an under-coat comb seasonally.

11

Here is a sampling of grooming tools and what they look like.

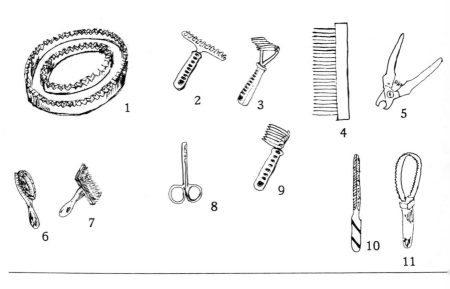

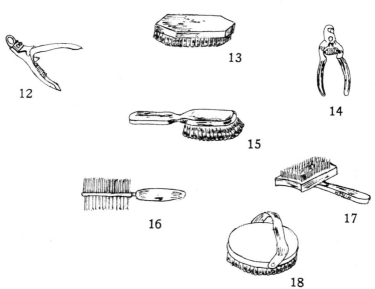

A SAMPLING OF TOOLS

1. Rubber palm brush
2. Undercoat comb
3. Large de-matting comb
4. Wide-toothed comb
5. Plier-type nail clipper
6. Pin brush
7. Fine wire slicker brush
8. Scissors-type nail clipper
9. Small de-matting comb
10. Nail file for dogs
11. Shedding rake
12. Guillotine-type nail clipper
13. Bristle brush
14. Another plier-type nail clipper
15. Another bristle brush
16. Double-sided comb
17. Curved slicker brush
18. Bristle palm brush

DOG ANATOMY

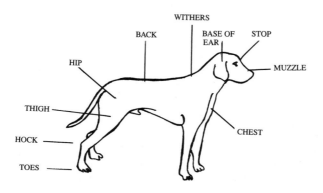

2 · THE GROOMING SESSION

Brushing

GENERAL TIPS

Tools: See "Breed and Brush Chart."

How To: (Remember: Take your dog outside to urinate before grooming and remove collar before you begin brushing)

Always begin brushing by smoothing your hands down to the end of his back. Start with his head and follow through down to the end of his back. You can think of this as a brief massage, as well as an opportunity for you to get a sense of your dog's coat and skin. With your hands you can feel if your dog is matted, if his coat seems dry, or if he seems to be shedding a lot. Repeat this action a few times. When you feel that your dog is calm, gently pick up the brush and begin brushing in the same manner.

Brush lightly at first, then increase the pressure so that you're brushing through the coat, but be careful not to dig into the skin. Start with the soft brush and switch to a stronger brush if you need to.

Begin at the neck and continue down the back to the hip area and lightly down the back legs. After the back legs are brushed, go on to the front legs, chest, rib cage, belly, and head (if it needs brushing).

Generally, there are three sensitive areas on your dog. The first is the hock (see illustration of dog anatomy). This is the small bone that protrudes on the back of your dog's leg. Never

14

brush this area hard with a wire slicker or pin brush. It will cause a brush burn that looks like a red scratch.

The second area to be careful of is the anus and genital area. If excrement is consistently getting stuck to the hair around your dog's anal area, a professional groomer can clip the hair there, making it easier for your dog to keep clean. Likewise, if there is a lot of hair getting tangled near the genital area, a professional groomer can trim it or clip it away.

And the third area that is sensitive for your dog is his face and ears. Some dogs will never need their face or ears brushed, but for poodles or long-haired dogs especially, you must see that this is done. Brush these areas last. Do not brush along the stop (see illustration on page 13), near the eyes, or on the nose. Some dogs will prefer a comb rather than a brush on their face, so try both to see which your dog prefers. Make sure you do not pull the skin underneath your dog's eyes while brushing or combing. Keep the thumb and forefinger of your non-working hand outstretched just below the eye in order to protect the eye area.

Grooming, in most cases, is common sense. Try to imagine the areas of your body that would be sensitive to brushing, and apply that to your dog. If you sense that your dog is particularly sensitive in one area, be very gentle when you brush there. It may simply be a sensitive spot for him, or perhaps there is something that is not readily apparent that is bothering him. Keep checking whenever you brush your dog to see if he requires a veterinarian's attention.

All dogs have at least one special sensitive spot, whether it be the front paws or the tail or the back end. Your dog may try to protect himself by biting on the brush. Go very easily and speak soothingly to him if he nips at the brush. When you sense that he is getting upset, return to an area that he enjoys having brushed. For most dogs, a safe place to return to is the back. Dogs usually love having their backs brushed. Then, once your dog is calm again, go back to the trouble spot and brush lightly and carefully so he learns not to be wary.

Brushing is a low-key, calming part of grooming. While brushing, remember to talk soothingly to your dog in a soft voice. You can tell him what happened at work or school, or what you are fixing for dinner—anything you want. Add a few

"What a good dog!" comments every once in a while and say his name lovingly. I like to make up little impromptu songs about the beautiful dog I am brushing. Dogs love to hear you sing. When grooming, always modulate your voice according to the activity you're involved in. For brushing, it should be low and calm. Save your excited exclamations for after the bath and final touches.

FOR SPECIFIC BREED TYPES

POODLE

When brushing poodle-type hair, you must brush the hair from the skin outward, so that the hair actually stands straight out. Brush a small section at a time, dividing the hair into sections, always working upward. To make things easier, place your non-brushing hand against the unbrushed hair so you can see the small section you are working on. Use brisk, light strokes and lift the hair instead of flattening it down.

Brush through the hair, alternating between the wire slicker and pin brushes. I like to start with the pin brush, then switch to the wire slicker. When you think you have your dog fairly well brushed out, carefully comb the hair to make sure all of the snags are out.

Combing Moose, a royal standard poodle, with a wide-toothed comb

Poodles require a lot of maintenance. To make things a little easier, you may want to keep your poodle in a moderately short puppy cut. (The puppy cut is a haircut in which all the hair is at one length so your dog resembles the way he looked as a puppy.) It looks great and will be easy for you to keep up at home.

TERRIER

Terriers are fairly easy to keep up because their hair rarely mats. Brush with the grain using only a fine wire slicker if they have long hair, or use a bristle brush if their hair is trimmed short. Make sure you brush the furnishings (longer hair on underbody and legs) since they can mat if not brushed. If your terrier or schnauzer has a long beard, be sure to brush and/or comb it often, as food tends to stick to the beard in little clumps.

Brushing Daisy, a wire fox terrier, with a wire brush

Long-haired large dogs require a great deal of brushing. If you are maintaining them in a full coat, it is best to brush them every day. Old English sheepdogs are especially prone to matting because of the thickness of their coats. If done on a daily basis, brushing can become second nature to both you and your dog. If it's difficult to brush the whole body every day, then try to break up the brushing into sections, front and back. Brush half of your dog at each session and brush him completely once or twice a week. The more you brush, the better your dog's coat will look and the easier the upkeep will be.

The most difficult time for brushing will be when your dog's coat changes from puppy to adult, anywhere from nine months to one and a half years of age. Every long-haired dog will go through a period during which the coat seems to be matting badly. Once the adult coat comes in, it will be coarser and easier to work with.

To brush, start with your pin brush. Part the dog's hair down the middle of his back and brush from the skin outward. When you come across a mat, use your wire slicker and a de-matting comb.

It is best to have your dog lie on his side when you're brushing the rib cage, legs, and underbelly. Since you will be brushing for a long time, let him change positions often in order for you to reach all the areas and to keep him from getting too restless.

When you are finished brushing, comb through your dog's coat with a wide-toothed comb. Go slowly and don't get too upset if you come across some small tangles. Should this happen, use your brush or de-matting comb and work the area again.

As your dog grows his adult coat, his hair will be long enough for a center part. After he is all brushed and combed out, start at the base of his head and use a comb to lightly separate his hair down the center of his back. You may want to use a light coat spray (see Chapter 4) to keep his hair in place during the first few attempts.

Center parts look great on Afghan hounds, briards, and

Combing Nanoosh's beard

bearded collies. Old English sheepdogs usually do not require a part. For "shaggy" mixed breeds, you can decide yourself whether to part them or not, or even whether to give them a shorter cut for easier maintenance. If you do not have the time to groom them daily, puppy cuts a few times a year are a nice alternative to keeping the hair long. Plan the puppy cut in the late spring before the sun is at its peak because dogs do get sunburned. It's not a good idea to cut them very short in the summer.

I will usually trim a dog in late April and then again in mid-September, since in New York, where I live, the weather becomes warm in May and stays warm often until late November. Speak with your professional groomer about when he or she feels is the best time for a short haircut in your particular climate.

LONG-HAIRED SMALL DOG

Long-haired small dogs require a lot of brushing, but because of their small stature, it is easy to get the job done in just one session. You will need the same tools that are required for long-haired large dogs, but in a smaller size.

Separate your dog's coat into sections and brush them from the skin outward. Brush the coat in layers starting from the back end and moving toward the front. If your dog is sporting a shorter cut, brush with the grain of the hair, then against the grain, and once more with the grain. For the tail, use the brush lightly so you don't take too much hair off of it. You may even try a bristle brush for the tail to keep it as full as possible.

Comb through the entire coat first with the wide-toothed comb, then switch to the fine-toothed comb for the finer hair. For most long-haired small dogs, draw a part along the back of the dog from head to tail. A center part will help keep the dog looking his best. Use a light coat dressing (see Chapter 4) to maintain the part during the first few groomings.

Brushing Hudson, a Lhaso apso puppy, against the grain

Use of a double-sided comb on Hudson

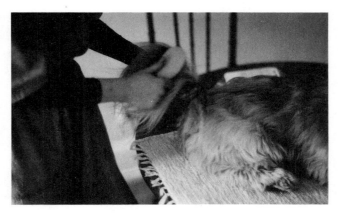

Be gentle when brushing tail

SILKY OR WIRY COAT WITH LIGHT FEATHERING

For dogs with a silky coat and feathers, you need to brush the feathers at least weekly (though more often, if your dog runs in the woods). The feathers will pick up any loose twigs, dried leaves, or other small particles which will cause the feathers to mat. Since the hair on the head and body is generally short, use a fine wire slicker brush on the body to pick up any dead hair. Use a pin brush on all of the feathers. Brush the feathers outward in the line of hair growth.

Most feathered dogs have hair on their ears. When brushing the ears, be careful not to brush with force. Lightly brush the ears with your pin brush, being especially careful at the ends of the ears where the skin is very thin. Hold the ear with your non-brushing hand and lightly brush through.

Comb through the feathers with a double-sided comb. On the legs, chest, and tail use the wider teeth. On the ears use the fine-toothed side. You can use a light coat dressing to bring out the shining on the coat if you wish.

SHORT-HAIRED DOG

For short-haired dogs, start brushing with the grain, then switch to brushing against the grain to loosen dead hair and dirt. Always finish with the grain of the hair.

For dogs that shed a lot, I have found that a small rake used for cats (or a rubber palm brush) will help to get rid of excess hair. Use very light strokes with the shedding rake, making sure not to hurt your dog.

Between the dog's baths you may want to apply a light coat spray while you brush to bring out the shine in his coat. Be very careful to spray well away from your dog's eyes, ears, and face. Hold the can six inches away from his coat and place your non-working hand over his eyes to protect them from the spray.

Use of a rubber palm brush on Vezna, a mixed breed

Chopka, a Rottweiler, waits his turn for brushing

DOUBLE-COATED DOG

Shedding out (the removal of the undercoat or "old coat") is required for all double-coated dogs and others who shed the undercoat seasonally. You will know by looking around your home if your dog needs to be shedded out. If you see hair everywhere, your dog is shedding. Take heart. When you groom your dog regularly, you will notice that he will shed heavily only at specific times of the year.

Though dogs will vary as to which month they will shed, most shedding takes place during spring and fall. It all depends on the climate, the temperature in your home, and the dog's own biological clock.

After shedding out his undercoat, your dog will look and feel better. The undercoat causes your dog to be uncomfortably warm, and gives him a haggard look. If the fur on your dog's back comes out easily when you pull on it gently, what you have in your hand is his undercoat or "old coat."

Using an undercoat comb or shedding rake, gently shed in the direction of your dog's hair. *Never* go against the grain while using a shedding brush, rake, or comb. It will break the hair. Always go with the grain and switch tools if your dog prefers one over the other. Certain tools work better on individual dogs regardless of their breed.

If you are using the rake, go very gently. Do not dig into your dog's back. When used correctly, the shedding comb, brush, or rake should feel like a great back scratcher. Remember, don't use any of the tools on the stomach, back of the legs, front legs, or, of course, the face or other sensitive areas.

Double-coated dogs should be brushed at least once every week with a pin brush or a wire slicker. Start by brushing with the grain, then go against the grain to loosen dead hair and dirt. Always finish by going with the grain to give the coat a glossy, finished look. Be careful brushing the tail, and never comb it with the shedding comb, as this will take out too much of the fullness. Dogs are very proud of their tails and brushing with a wire slicker brush will be enough to take out the undercoat while maintaining the bulk of the tail.

Brushing Selma, a border collie

MATS

In brushing, one should always be careful of matted areas. When you come across a mat, place your non-working hand between the dog's skin and the mat, and gently brush the mat without any pressure on your dog's skin. If the mat is large, try to separate it with your fingers by slowly pulling it apart. As you loosen it, use a comb or brush to unravel it more.

It is best to get out all of the matting before you give your dog a bath because water will tighten the mat, making it worse when it dries. If your dog is not too badly matted, you can saturate the mats with a de-tangler and let it sit for a few minutes before the bath. But this should only be done for mild cases and only right before a bath. If your dog is extremely matted, I suggest taking him to a professional groomer for stripping down (cutting the hair short). Once this has been done, you can start from the beginning with good brushing habits as the new coat comes in.

For de-matting, a de-matting comb is a useful tool. Follow the rules above, using the comb to separate the hair and remembering to always protect your dog with your non-working hand to keep the skin from being pulled. Never use the de-matting comb against the grain, and be careful not to dig into your dog's skin. You can hold the hair above the mat very tightly and lightly rake the mat until it begins to pull apart. Then use a wire slicker and the larger part of a double-sided comb to take out the dead hair that is tangled in the mat.

De-matting is a slow process, but once accomplished, brushing daily will prevent mats from forming again. If you feel that your long-haired dog is too much to keep up by yourself, consult a professional groomer. A shorter cut or trim may be what's needed to help make your dog more comfortable.

Hold the matted hair between your dog's skin and the mat

Clipping Toenails

Clipping toenails is painless when done correctly. What makes it difficult at times is that some dogs do not like their paws held, especially their front paws. I haven't figured out why, but terriers are notorious for this.

Locating the dew claw

In clipping, it's always a good idea to do the job as quickly as you can, being careful not to take off too much nail. Reward your dog with his favorite treat after clipping his toenails, so that he comes to think of it as a simple, pleasurable experience. Just in case you cut a bit too much of the nail, have on hand a small bottle of cut stop or a styptic pencil to stop any bleeding. Ideally, you won't have to use it.

There is a vein and nerve called the quick running down the center of your dog's nail, and if the quick is cut, it will bleed and cause discomfort. On light-colored nails, it is easy to see the quick. You will notice a red part of the nail and you'll want to clip below that. (You're simply trying to cut off the hooked part of the nail.) On black nails, right before the quick, you will see a small white dot in the center of the nail. If you see this, the correct amount of nail has been cut off.

It is best to clip off just a little of the nail and keep them up every month. The wonderful thing about a dog's nails is that when you cut off a little, the quick will retract. This will allow you to shorten your dog's nails over a period of several months, each month taking off a little bit more.

You may not need to cut the back nails as much as the front ones, as they tend to wear down more frequently, particularly if your dog walks or runs on concrete.

Some dogs have dew claws, which are located on the inside of their front legs around the wrist area (they may occasionally appear on the back legs). These nails must always be cut since they have no way of wearing down by themselves. If they are not cut, they will grow into themselves (resembling a ram's horn) and will eventually cause pain and swelling.

If your dog's dew claw has reached this point, don't worry. Just use a plier-type clipper and put a little hydrogen peroxide on the skin surrounding the dew claw.

Tools:

For small dogs: small guillotine-type clipper

For medium to large dogs: large guillotine-type clipper

For very large dogs: plier-type clipper

Cut stop or styptic pencil

Emery board or nail file for dogs

NOTE: *Never use a nail clipper meant for people on your dog.*

How To:

If your dog is standing, begin by holding the back paw in a straight line in back of him. Never pull your dog's legs out to the side! They are not built for that movement. While you are holding your dog's paw in your non-working hand with the front part of his paw gently resting in your palm, lightly press the pad of his paw to allow for a better view of his nails. Using the guillotine-type clipper either frontways or sideways, quickly snip off just the hooked part of the nail.

To clip the front nails, it is best if your dog is sitting down. Gently lift the front paw in front of your dog (straight out, never to the side) and again hold his paw in your non-working hand. Gently press the pad for a good view of the nail and quickly snip off the hooked part.

If you do cut too close to the quick and it starts to bleed, don't panic. Just put a little cut stop on the nail and press for a few seconds. That should stop the bleeding. Apologize to your dog and give him a hug, telling him you will try not to do that again.

If your dog is elderly and needs to be lying on his side, simply position yourself next to him, take up his paw (straight, never to the side), press the pad lightly, and clip.

After clipping, you may want to file your dog's nails to take away the sharp edges. Use a file meant only for dogs and file in one direction. If you are using an emery board, you can file lightly in both directions. If a dog's nails are properly filed, they will be less likely to scratch people and furniture. This is especially true for dogs who spend a lot of time indoors.

Filing Daisy's nail with an emery board

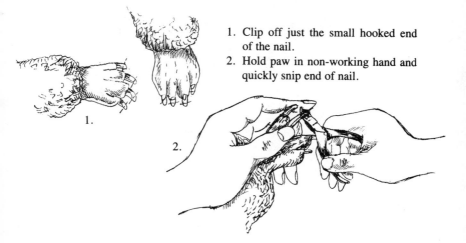

1. Clip off just the small hooked end of the nail.
2. Hold paw in non-working hand and quickly snip end of nail.

Ears are a common place for infections to start and dirt to build up. Cleaning your dog's ears once a month is good preventive health care. The ears are also a place where ticks love to hide, so it is particularly important to check your dog's ears in the spring and summer.

Most dogs love to have their ears cleaned. If there is a lot of hair in your dog's ears (as is the case with poodles and long-haired dogs), ask a professional groomer to clean the hair out for you. *Never* use a Q-tip® or cotton swab in your dog's ear. Use only a cotton ball.

If you notice a lot of debris or a rancid odor in your dog's ears, or if he has been scratching the area a lot, see your veterinarian. Chances are he has either an ear infection or ear mites. Both are best treated by your veterinarian. But if your dog's ears are just dirty, that's where you come in.

Tools:

a mixture of alcohol and hydrogen peroxide (three parts to one) or you can use just alcohol

cotton balls

Cleaning Daisy's ear

How To:

Always clean the inside of the ear first. Saturate a cotton ball with the alcohol mixture and squeeze out any excess. Lightly wipe the inside of your dog's ear without digging into the inner ear. Turn the cotton ball over and gently rub the inside of the long part of the ear to clean away any dirt that has accumulated there.

After cleaning your dog's ear, massage the base of his ear lightly with your thumb and forefinger. Dogs love having their ears massaged. Next, go on to his other ear, always using a new cotton ball. Never go from one ear to another or from one dog to another with the same cotton ball, for you may inadvertently transmit an infection. To prevent infection, never wash the inside of the ear with water during the bath.

After you are finished, take an extra minute to massage both ears and give your dog another treat before moving on to another stage of grooming.

The Teeth

Teeth are usually the most neglected part of grooming and preventive health care. Most people laugh when I tell them to buy their dog a toothbrush and occasionally to brush their dog's teeth. But keeping your dog's teeth in good shape is very easy and also important.

It is easier to start brushing your dog's teeth when he is a puppy, but it is worth a try to start brushing them at any age. I started brushing Syd's teeth when she was eight years old, and she was very tolerant of the procedure.

Dogs rarely get cavities, but their teeth do build up tartar, which left unattended will cause the gums to weaken and the teeth to eventually fall out. "Doggie breath" is an indication of tartar buildup. Hard dog biscuits, a kibble-type dry dog food, rawhide sticks and bones, and sterilized bones (obtained at your pet shop) all help to prevent tartar from forming.

It is important to check your dog's teeth monthly and to brush them, if needed, every week. If your dog's teeth are too small for a toothbrush, use a sterilized pad instead. Never use toothpaste made for people on your dog, for it will upset his stomach.

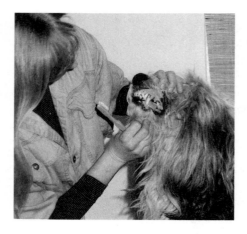
Lift skin above teeth line to expose teeth for brushing. Your dog will only appear to look mean

Tools:

soft child's toothbrush or sterilized pad

a paste made of baking soda and water, or toothpaste for dogs

How To:

Place a small amount of baking soda paste (or toothpaste for dogs) on the toothbrush. Since tartar will mostly form on the outside surfaces of your dog's teeth, we are most concerned with brushing only the outside. It is not important to unclench your dog's teeth, but rather use one hand to raise his upper lip gently to expose the surface of his upper teeth and the other hand to lightly brush each tooth. Be careful not to brush your dog's gums. Gently pull at the corner of his mouth to expose his back teeth. Do not dig or scrub too hard. If you notice that there is a large tartar buildup or if any of your dog's teeth seem loose, consult your veterinarian.

The Eyes

Dogs, like people, build up "sleep" in the corners of their eyes. Dogs differ on how much will build up, though long-haired dogs and poodles seem to have the most buildup. If your dog has a lot of buildup, you may want to have a professional groomer trim around the eyes to help you maintain cleanliness.

Wiping your dog's eyes is simple and takes very little time.

Tools:

your gentle hands (be careful of long nails)

a washcloth or cotton ball with warm water

How To:

I find it most gentle to use both hands at once. While resting your dog's muzzle in both hands, gently wipe below the corner of his eyes with your thumbs. If tears are caked up, use a washcloth or cotton ball and warm water. Cleaning eyes is the simplest part of grooming and your dog's eyes should be checked daily.

The Bath

The bath is a favorite time for me because it gives me the opportunity to pamper a dog to the fullest. It is important for you to be totally in charge of your dog in the bath and to continually soothe and reassure him about how wonderful the bath is. Dogs love their bath when you love it with them. They feel so refreshed after it's over that you and your dog both know it was worth the effort.

The bath is a time for scratching and massaging, singing to your dog, and being kind to him. Treat him like a baby and he will love the bath as much as a baby does.

Make sure the bath area is warm. While bathing your dog, don't run an air conditioner or allow any drafts to come in from a window. Use a rubber mat in the sink or tub so your dog won't lose his balance and fall. You may want to have a towel spread out on the floor or counter area for your dog to step on so he doesn't slip. Encourage big dogs (but not older ones) to get into the tub themselves. Usually a treat will help them get the idea the first few times.

Veterinarians used to say that bathing dries out the coat, but a dry coat is really an indication of several other factors. One such factor in the winter is dry heat. Dry heat in your home or apartment can deplete your dog's coat of its natural oils. If you use a high-quality dog shampoo and creme rinse, though, oil will be restored to the coat and skin.

Flea shampoo will also dry out your dog's coat. I suggest, when using a flea shampoo, to use a creme rinse to counterbalance the effects of the drying chemicals in the shampoo. (Creme rinse and certain coat sprays can also help alleviate the problem of flaky skin, which some dogs are prone to.) Every dog, like every person, has his own tendency toward dry skin. If your dog has a tendency to be drier in the winter, use a bit more creme rinse or try a shampoo designed especially for dry or flaky skin.

Never use a shampoo made for people, with the exception of baby shampoo. Dog shampoos are gentler for a dog's skin and they have the correct pH balance, which differs from shampoos for people.

Keep a gentle but firm hand on withers while bathing

Always protect your dog's eyes and ears from the water

Tools:

bath or sink mat

detachable shower head or hose attachment for sink or tub

shampoo and creme rinse (see Chapter 4)

washcloth (for washing the face of a dog who has short hair on his face)

towels

Precautions (optional):

To protect your dog's eyes from shampoo or water, you may want to place a drop of mineral oil in each eye. If your dog is prone to eye infection, use an ophthalmic bacitracin ointment to protect his eyes. (Before doing this, consult your veterinarian.)

To protect your dog's ears from shampoo or water, use a cotton ball in each ear. (Again, consult your veterinarian for his or her opinion about this precaution.)

Never point the water/shower hose in the direction of your dog's eyes, ears, or face.

Preparation:

Did you remember to let your dog outside to urinate before you began grooming?

Place mat in tub or sink.

Have the shower hose ready to use.

Clear away all unnecessary objects from the sink or tub. Never leave glass bottles around the grooming area.

Have two or three towels close at hand (and you may want an extra one for the floor).

Have your dog's favorite treat on hand.

Leave yourself a half-hour to forty minutes of uninterrupted time.

Always use lukewarm to warm water for the bath; not hot, not cold. If you are bathing your dog outside, make sure both hot and cold water are available.

How To:

Begin by placing your dog in the sink or tub, though you want to encourage a large dog to jump in himself. With the hose facing away from the dog, turn on the cold water. Slowly add the hot water until you reach a lukewarm to warm temperature.

Now, begin to wet down your dog completely. (Try to keep one hand on your dog's back at all times for support.) If he tries to shake the water off, gently but with authority place a hand on his upper back (withers). This will stop him from shaking off the water and shampoo before you are done.

After he is totally wet, begin to apply the shampoo. Put a little shampoo in the palm of your hand and rub it on your dog's back. As with brushing, always shampoo your dog's face last. If he is short-haired on the face, you can use a washcloth, gently smoothing the damp cloth over his head and down his muzzle. For a long-haired face, gently shampoo the hair in the direction of hair growth so it doesn't tangle and rinse immediately. Don't leave shampoo on his face. Should your dog shake, you don't want even a tearless shampoo to get into his eyes.

Make sure you have shampooed the entire body. You may have to shampoo the feet, inside the pads, and the outside paws more than once to get those areas really clean.

I generally shampoo the back of a dog, the tail, the under-side, and legs first. Leaving the shampoo on those areas, I then go to the face, completely washing and rinsing it. Then I return to massaging the shampoo into the dog's entire body.

Use your fingers alternately to massage and scrub (without tangling) your dog's fur. Most dogs will relish having their backs scratched as you shampoo them. Let them enjoy this to the fullest. Keep in mind that this is a day at the spa for your friend.

Always be careful with the water. Never wash inside your dog's ears with water. Water trapped in the ears can lead to infection. You can wash the outside of the ear of long-eared dogs by cupping your non-working hand over the ear. For short-eared dogs, just use a damp washcloth on the outside of their ears.

Be very careful when washing dogs who have "bulging eyes," like the Lhasa apso, Shih Tzu, or Pekingese. Do not get

Remember to talk to your dog while bathing him. Eye contact is important

any shampoo or water near the eye area and never pull the hair or skin on the face either downward or upward away from the eyes. The eyes of these dogs are very sensitive.

Once the shampooing is done, rinse completely. It is very important to get all of the shampoo out, for it will dry the skin if left in.

After your dog is clean and all the shampoo is rinsed out, it is time to apply creme rinse (see Chapter 4 for a suggested brand). To do this, place a small amount in the palm of your hand and rub your palms together so the creme rinse is on both hands. Now, lightly massage it into your dog's coat, starting from the withers downward to his tail. Then place a little more creme rinse in your hands and apply to his chest.

For long-haired dogs, apply enough creme rinse to cover the entire coat. Use your judgment on how much you will need to use. To rinse, use lukewarm to warm water, and starting with the withers, rinse the creme rinse through the coat. With some creme rinses, you can leave a residue in. Always read the label for complete instructions. Use creme rinse on all dogs except poodles, bichon frises, and Bedlington terriers.

After rinsing out the creme rinse, turn off the water and grab a towel. Take your hand off your dog's back and let him shake off. When he does, say, "Good dog!" Shaking off is wonderful. You can hold a towel in front of yourself to keep from getting wet, but always reward your dog for shaking off. It's still the best way for him to rid himself of excess water, and it also allows him some freedom after staying still so long in the tub.

Before allowing your dog out of the tub, use both hands to squeeze the excess water from his body and legs. Gently rub down the legs, getting as much water out as you can. Repeat with each leg a few times. Now help your dog out of the tub. He will probably shake off more. Encourage and reward him.

Dogs become very perky after a bath. Before letting him run around, take a towel and, starting with the face, lightly begin to dry him. As you are toweling him dry, advance to vigorous strokes on his back, telling him how wonderful and clean he is. This is the time for your most demonstrative "What a good dog!" comments.

With long-haired dogs, do not swirl the towel or you will create mats. Towel in the direction of the hair. With short-haired dogs and terriers, feel free to stroke and towel away. Using the towel with both hands, vigorously rub your dog's back, being sure to go lightly on sensitive areas. If you are toweling a small delicate dog or an older dog, be gentle and use your discretion on how hard to rub.

After your dog is towel-dried, you may want to let him have a short break before blow-drying him and brushing him out. Let him run around the apartment or house for a few minutes. It will make blow-drying quicker and it will give you and your dog a chance to collect yourselves.

Blow-Drying and Brushing

After towel-drying, the last step in grooming is blow-drying, brushing and/or shedding out. For all dogs, it is a good idea to let them get used to the blow-dryer. Most dogs will be startled by the noise at first, but soon they'll come to like being blow-dried. Here again, it is up to you to make blow-drying a calm, easy experience for your dog.

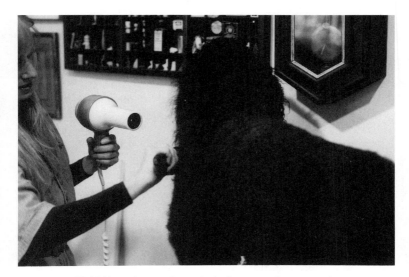

Hold blow-dryer at least six inches away from your dog

Blow-drying is not always necessary. If it's summer and it's warm outside, you may want to let your dog dry outside before brushing him out. Use your common sense.

Tools:

Check the chart on page 11 for the type of brush, comb, and shedding tool you will need for your dog.

a blow dryer with two or more settings

a towel (optional) for your dog to lie on

Precautions:

Make sure you and your dog are not standing or sitting on a wet surface.

Mop up and get rid of all the water on the floor before plugging in the blow-dryer.

Never put the blow-dryer directly on your dog; hold it at least six inches away from him at all times.

Do not use high heat.

Keep the blow-dryer moving while in use. Do not hold it in one spot for too long.

Never aim the blow-dryer at your dog's sensitive areas, eyes, inside the ears, or face.

Preparation:

First sit with your dog and gently begin to brush him, getting a sense of his hair. Turn on the blow-dryer at a low setting with your non-working hand. Now, as you rest your working hand on your dog's back for his security, keep the blow-dryer at arm's length behind you. Speak soothingly to your dog. Before aiming the blow-dryer in your dog's direction, allow him to get used to the sound of it for a minute or so. Then point the dryer in your direction to show him that you aren't afraid of it. Talk to him in a calming manner.

How To:

As with most areas of grooming, begin with your dog's back. Hold the blow-dryer in your non-working hand and brush with your working hand. Lift your dog's hair away from the blow-dryer to achieve a fluffy look.

Generally, it's best to blow-dry your dog's hair in sections. Start with his back and then go slowly on to his hip area and down his legs. If your dog has very little hair on his legs, you can simply towel-dry them. Concentrate on the wettest area. Obviously, long-haired dogs will need the most blow-drying.

Remember to take precautions with the dryer and turn it off from time to time to give your dog and yourself a rest. This will save wear and tear on the dryer as well.

If it is winter, make sure your dog is completely dry before going outside. If it is warm out, it's all right for your short-haired dog to be a little damp when going outside. But long-haired dogs must be completely dry or else they will mat up outside.

Since you have brushed your dog before bathing him, brushing after the bath is easier. Follow the same rules as before and brush slightly outward when possible. For poodles, always

Brush the hair upward and outward as you blow-dry

brush and blow-dry in an upward motion to create a beautiful, fluffy look. Comb through long-haired dogs and poodles after blow-drying, but do not use the comb with the blow-dryer.

Praise

After you are finished brushing and drying, it is time for lavish praise! You and your dog have earned it. If the grooming area has a door, put down all the tools (always unplug your blow-dryer!), and let your dog out of the room first. It is time for treats and many "What a beautiful dog!" or "What a good dog!" comments. If there are other family members or friends in the house, everyone should stop what they're doing and comment on how beautiful your dog looks.

Once you are done, stop. Never make your dog come back for one last grooming stroke or one last tidbit. Save it for next time. Now is the time only for praise and adulation. There is always next time for perfection, and perfection is not in the least bit important anyway.

Optional Finishes

BOWS

You may want to consider putting a bow or barrette in your dog's hair. If your dog is in full coat and a bow suits him, it is a fun way to prepare him for a party. A bow may also be useful simply to keep the hair out of his eyes (if he is a Lhasa apso, for example).

1. Top knot bows
2. Side bow

Tools:

small barrettes

rubber band with bow (available at pet shops)

a small piece of seam binding lace in a pretty color (makes a great bow without a rubber band)

comb

How To:

For a top knot, part your dog's hair on his head in a small triangular shape. Use the inside corner of your dog's eye as a starting point and make a small line going backward. Do the same on the other side, and then make a part for the back line. If this isn't enough hair, use the middle of the eye as a starting point. Now place the barrette or bow in his hair.

Another way of dressing up your dog is by putting two small bows on either side of his head. Make a part down the middle of your dog's head and section off a very petite ponytail on either side. Add the bows or barrettes. *Don't* pull the hair too tightly or you will stretch the skin above the ears.

3 · ADVICE AND HINTS

How you approach grooming your dog is the key to good grooming. Think of yourself as your dog's personal stylist, masseuse, hairdresser, dentist, manicurist, and visiting nurse all rolled into one. When you groom, you work on the entire body of the animal from head to toe.

A great joy in grooming is visualizing before and after pictures of your dog. You will notice a great change in your dog after he is groomed. Look at the way he walks. After a bath, a dog seems to prance around as if he were a Hollywood star.

Don't be frustrated if it seems difficult at first. As with any new venture, it takes practice to become a deft and skilled groomer. If you are afraid of one element of grooming, ask a friend or family member to help you. If you are unsure about cutting nails, for example, ask your veterinarian or professional groomer to help you. Don't let any one facet of grooming turn you off to the entire experience. Go slowly and you will build confidence in yourself and in your dog.

Attitude

A good attitude is most important in preparing both you and your dog for grooming. Grooming is a loving and caring gift for your dog. If you dread it, so will your animal. If you are happy about grooming and love your clean and beautiful dog, he will learn to enjoy the experience as much as he enjoys food or play.

In fact, there is time for both food and play during the grooming session.

After cutting nails, a special liver treat may be just the right thing to develop a positive feeling. After a bath, words of praise and a nice rubdown with a towel feel great. Massage helps alleviate stress and promotes a good feeling about grooming. Use massage to move from one part of grooming to another. Before and after brushing, smooth your dog's coat from head to tail.

Dogs feel most comfortable when the groomer is in control of the situation. Always try to keep one hand gently but firmly on your dog's back. If he seems squirmy or wiggly at first (which is especially the case with puppies), give him time to run around before and after his bath.

And a reminder—make sure he's had the chance to go to the bathroom before the grooming session.

Consistency

Consistency helps your dog get used to the grooming experience and also helps keep him in his best condition. Try to keep your dog's grooming on a fairly regular schedule. If he is not feeling well, let his bath go. Still, you might want to brush him gently. The more closely you stick to a schedule, the better your dog will look and the easier it will be for him to get used to grooming. Consistent grooming makes for calmer dogs who will be able to handle new experiences and new people better.

Different Ages

Dogs of all ages benefit from home grooming. As long as you are sensitive to your dog's stage in life, grooming will be fun and rewarding. Whether you are grooming a four-month-old puppy or a fourteen-year-old dog, patience is the key.

A puppy requires time to sniff all of the tools and to adjust to staying in one place while you groom him. Make the early grooming sessions particularly fun for him and allow him some puppy mischief. Each time you groom your puppy, demand a little bit more from him, but always maintain a gentle, positive attitude.

Grooming an older dog who has never been groomed before is a little bit trickier than grooming a puppy, but just as rewarding. Older dogs require great sensitivity to adjust to new tasks or situations. Like dogs of all ages, they need to feel wanted and appreciated, and grooming helps them to feel loved and beautiful.

In some cases, older dogs have a weakness in their back legs which makes it difficult for them to stand for very long. Brush them while they are lying comfortably on their side. They can even lie down in the bathtub for most of the soaping and scrubbing.

The aftereffects of a bath for an older dog are truly heartwarming. They do feel more like young dogs again and their ailments from old age seem to disappear, at least for a while.

Be kind to your dog no matter what his age. Grooming is not about perfection, it is only a means for your dog to feel and look his best. Grooming will enhance your dog's life and, ideally, your tender loving care will add years to it as well.

4 · PRODUCT SUGGESTIONS

Shampoos

Here's a list of shampoos, creme rinses, and coat sprays that I have found to be particularly good. If you are happy with the products you are currently using, then by all means continue to use them. I suggest, however, that you switch off occasionally with whatever you're using. A change in shampoo, for instance, may perk up your dog's coat. Keep abreast of new products for dogs and try them out to see if they make a positive difference. *Remember,* never use a shampoo designed for people on your dog.

ALL DOGS

1. Coat Brightener Shampoo™ for dogs by Oster

   (excellent all-purpose shampoo)

WHITE DOGS

1. Bright White Shampoo by Ring 5 (tearless)

   (great for white poodles, bichon frises, and for use in conjunction with another shampoo on the faces and feet of Old English sheepdogs, bearded collies, and other dogs where you want the white to stand out)

BLACK DOGS

1. Black Sheen Shampoo™ by Hagen

   (great for bringing back the black when dogs such as black poodles, etc., are starting to gray)

   NOTE: This product may be drying to some coats in winter; use only occasionally.

GOLDEN DOGS

1. Pure Gold Shampoo by Pro-Line

   (excellent for gold-colored dogs, especially Lhasa apsos, golden retrievers, wheaten terriers, and briards)

FOR FLAKY SKIN AND DRY HAIR

1. Organic formula 60 with bee pollen and aloe vera by Lightning

   (excellent for dogs who have skin irritations due to fleas and also good for flaky skin and dry hair)

2. Good Bye Dry Conditioning Shampoo™ by Lambert Kay (with aloe and lanolin)

It's a good idea to use either of these shampoos after the flea season to restore your dog's coat after using a flea and tick shampoo. No matter how gentle a flea shampoo is, it still has chemicals that will dry out your dog's coat to varying degrees. Also, if your dog has been swimming in either a lake or salt water, or even in a pool, be sure to use a shampoo for dry hair to restore his coat.

Creme Rinse

I use only one creme rinse because I have had such wonderful results with it. I like it because it doesn't flatten down the hair like many creme rinses; it is a reconstructor which enhances the look and feel of your dog's coat.

1. Blair's Satin Beauty Hair Treatment & Reconstructor for Show Dogs and Show Cats

This can be used on any dog except poodles, bichon frises, and Bedlington terriers. For these dogs, do not use a creme rinse. If your dog is very matted, use a de-tangler before his bath.

Detangler

1. Untangle by Ring 5 (to use before the bath)

Coat Sprays

To spruce up your dog in between bath times, and to help add sheen to his coat as you brush, you may want to try the following:

1. Show Groom Conditioner® with sunscreen, mink oil, and vitamin E by Mr. Groom
2. Vitamin E Enriched Super Mink Oil Spray® with sun shield by Bio Groom

(Both of these sprays are good protection from the sun, particularly for clipped dogs living in sunny climates.)

3. Canine Coat Conditioner™ with lanolin and protein by *(also helps eliminate mats)* Pro Groom

Be careful when using a spray to keep it well away from your dog's eyes, ears, and face. Keep your non-working hand over your dog's eyes as you spray from the withers downward. Do not spray near his anus or genitals, since all sprays have alcohol in them which can burn sensitive areas.

Callouses and Cracked Pads

1. Vitamin E Skin Cream (E-6000) by Mason Natural
2. Protecta-Pad for dry and cracking pads by Tomlyn

Treats and Rewards

I suggest that you use a special treat just for grooming rewards. This will help your dog to have a positive association with grooming. Whichever treat you use, never use it to mask medication. Dogs have a keen sense of smell and will associate that particular treat with medicine.

1. 100% Freeze-Dried Liver® by Redi

2. Small pieces of American cheese

(NOTE: Use both of these treats in moderation since they are delicious, but very rich.)

3. Meaty Bones®

4. Milk Bones®

5. Iams Biscuits®

(These are also good for preventing tartar.)

5 • SPECIAL SITUATIONS OR PROBLEMS

FLEAS

Fleas, ticks, and mites are all parasites, and unfortunately all dogs and dog owners will probably come across them at some point in their lives. It is important to treat any parasite problem immediately because untreated, they create further problems and discomfort for your dog.

Fleas feed on your dog's blood. They do not fly, but jump from one dog or cat to another, where the female flea lays her eggs. Once infested with fleas, your dog must be treated, as should your home, especially the areas where your dog has been, and any other animals who live there.

Some dogs are allergic to the flea's saliva. Your dog may lose his hair and develop bloody patches called hot spots where he has scratched and bitten himself. If he swallows a flea, he may develop tapeworm. So the sooner you treat this problem, the better.

To Check for Fleas:

If your dog is consistently scratching in one area, this is a good indication that fleas are present. Part your dog's hair where he is scratching and observe the area. Fleas are tiny brown insects and may be very difficult to see. On light-colored dogs, it is easy to see flea feces, which look like little black flecks of dirt and will turn red when wet. If your dog is dark in color, you may want to rub his skin and hair, then shake off any matter onto a piece of white paper for a better inspection.

How to Rid Your Dog of Fleas:

Using a flea shampoo, follow the directions for a regular bath with these precautions:

Be extremely careful of your dog's eye area. Make sure you read all of the directions on the bottle of the flea shampoo and follow them to the letter. If it says to be careful of specific areas of your dog, be sure to do so. If your dog is a puppy, be sure to get a flea shampoo specifically designed for puppies. If your dog is pregnant or lactating, consult your veterinarian before giving her a flea bath.

Never mix chemicals. If you have just given your dog a flea bath, wait a few days before you put on a flea collar or flea powder. *Always check with your veterinarian to see if the flea products you are using are compatible.*

It is best to leave flea dipping (in which the dog is saturated with a chemical to destroy the fleas) to a professional groomer or your veterinarian since the chemicals used are much stronger than those contained in ordinary flea shampoo.

For all flea shampoos, the shampoo must stay on your dog for several minutes before being washed off. Make sure you pay attention to the time in order for the shampoo to work best. Keep a firm hand on your dog's withers so he does not shake any of the shampoo into his eyes.

Also, see to it that the shampoo reaches the inside of the back legs. Fleas love to hide there. Rinse off with extra care. You may apply a light creme rinse, if you desire. Lastly, clean your dog's ears as described earlier (see Chapter 2) to make sure you've reached any fleas hiding there. *Remember:* If your dog is infested with fleas, you must also spray or bomb your home in order to rid the area of fleas and to prevent a recurrence.

TICKS

Ticks are also a common nuisance. They are usually found in marshy or wooded areas. It is particularly important to check your dog for ticks during the warmer months of the year.

Ticks are small parasites that feed on your dog's blood. They are usually easier to see when they are engorged with blood. They are small grayish blobs when engorged. If you see a tick, be sure to remove it as soon as possible, and once you have done so, check to see if there are any more. Ticks particularly like the ears, face, arm pits, and the tail area of your dog, so check these places first. Your dog may not give you any indication that he has ticks, so it is up to you to check him.

Tools:

    tweezers

    alcohol

    Vaseline

How To:

The fastest way to remove a tick is to use a tweezer. It is extremely important that you remove the head of the tick, which is embedded in your dog's skin. This means you will be going into your dog's skin a little bit in order to remove the head. If the head is left in, it will create a sore on your dog, so always remove the whole tick.

Once you have removed the tick, destroy it. If they are not destroyed, ticks will continue to seek a host. After removal, place a drop of alcohol on your dog where the tick was. Then blow on your dog's skin where you placed the alcohol as you would with a child's scrape.

If the tick is close to your dog's eye or another place where using a tweezer is not a good idea, Vaseline may be used.

Take a good quantity of Vaseline and place it around and over the tick. This will smother the tick and cause it to retract. When it retracts, remove it with your fingers and destroy it. Again, make sure you have removed the entire tick.

There is a wonderful tool called a tick remover, but it can be hard to find. Ask the people at your local pet shop if they have heard of it and where you might purchase one. *Never* use kerosene or a lighted match to remove a tick from your dog. They are both liable to burn your dog's skin.

SUNBURN

Many people don't realize that dogs, like people, can become sunburned from long exposure to the sun. That's why it's best to clip your dog short before the summer begins. If your dog is sporting a short cut and will be out in the sun for extended periods of time, you can help him by using a coat conditioner with sunscreen (see Chapter 4). You can tell if your dog is becoming sunburned if you notice that his skin looks particularly pink on a center part or where there is a sparseness of hair. If your dog is outside a lot during the summer months, it is also a good idea to make sure he has plenty of water and a shady place to rest. When dogs get older, they seem to prefer the shade most of the time.

Winter

During the winter, it is important to try to steer your dog away from the salt that is put down to melt ice in many places. This is particularly difficult if you live in the city, since salt is used often to clear sidewalks and streets.

Salt will burn your dog's sensitive pads. Also, if your dog licks the salt off of his pads, the corrosive salt gets into his digestive tract, and that can be dangerous.

So, every time you take your dog out where there is salt, you must wash his feet with a warm wet washcloth and a very little bit of soap once you're home again. Most dogs will get the hang of feet washing after you have done it a few times. Our dogs will wait patiently by the door during the winter months until we wipe their feet.

Quickly and gently wipe each foot inside the pads where the salt usually will sting the most and get caught. Don't use too much soap, and make sure not to leave any soap in the pads or on the feet.

If your dog's pads are cracking in the winter, use a vitamin

E cream to help the skin heal. Check with the people at your pet shop for a special cream for cracked pads (see Chapter 4).

Some dogs are very sensitive to the ice and salt in winter. Most dogs I know do not particularly like rubber boots, but there are new boots made of soft leather that attach to a coat or sweater with suspenders that dogs seem to like a little better. If your dog's feet are very sensitive, it is worth trying leather boots. It will make winter more pleasant for him.

Some dogs will need a sweater or coat in winter. It is crucial for small dogs always to wear a sweater or coat outside because they can develop chest colds if they're not kept adequately warm. Small dogs are more prone to getting cold than larger dogs because their slight stature offers little resistance to the elements and they are very close to the ground, which adds to their discomfort.

Generally speaking, any dog under twenty pounds is a potential candidate for a coat or sweater in winter. Older large dogs may also feel better if they have a light sweater for particularly chilly days. Consult your veterinarian for his or her thoughts on this issue for your particular dog.

One note here on winter hiking or camping with your dog: Dogs can get hypothermia and it is very important if you take your dog on winter trips outside that he has a warm blanket to sleep on or a warm sleeping bag. I took Syd camping in the fall when she was two years old, and when it was time to sleep, I fully expected her to want to sleep on the ground, but she preferred to share my sleeping bag since she became chilled at nightfall. From that time on, I always brought a warm blanket for her.

It is also very important to bring several large towels on a camping trip when your dog is with you, because if he finds a stream to wade in, it is important that you dry him extremely well before the sun goes down.

Remember, dogs are domesticated and are not suited to the wilds. They love to romp around in the cold winter air as long as they have a warm place in which to rest away from the cold and wind. If your dog is outside for most of the day, make sure he has access to a warm, dry place if he needs it and definitely a warm place to sleep in at night.

CALLUSES

Sometimes on large short-haired dogs you may notice a callus forming on the elbows or hocks. This is caused by the pressure on the joint without padding. If your dog is still a puppy, you can deter a callus from forming by rubbing vitamin E cream into the elbow joint, hock, or any other joints that your dog tends to place a lot of his weight on.

If your dog already has a callus formed, use vitamin E cream often, rubbing it into the callus. It will also help to have a soft, thick rug or blanket in your dog's lounging and sleeping area.

If You Have More Than One Dog

If you have two or more dogs, it is best if they are bathed on the same day. Dogs will get confused if all of a sudden their friend smells different. Bathing only one dog may also cause fights to erupt since they may feel they have to reestablish the delicate balance in their hierarchy. One dog could also get jealous if he feels he is being left out of a special event.

Even if you have one short-haired dog and one long-haired one, pay attention to both of them. It is not the amount of time you spend with each dog that is important, it is your sensitivity to their need for attention that counts. You may have to spend an hour with your sheepdog and only ten minutes with your dalmatian when brushing, but it doesn't matter. What's important is that you take the time with both of them. Since your sheepdog will require a bath every month, I suggest you keep your dalmatian on the same schedule. It won't hurt him and this way he won't feel neglected.

When I am doing a full grooming session on more than one dog, I will switch from one dog to another when I feel one may need a rest or the other is getting jealous. Try to accomplish a few of the basics on each dog before switching. Try to clean the ears, clip the nails, clean the teeth, and begin to brush before switching to the second dog. If one dog doesn't like a grooming task, or if they both like one task in particular, switch back and forth. Much depends on you and your dogs.

You should usually groom a senior dog before grooming a puppy, since the puppy is new to grooming. If your older dog likes grooming, he will be teaching your puppy how much fun it can be.

It is always a good idea to bathe one dog after another. You can have both dogs in the room or just one in the room, but don't put both dogs in the tub at the same time. Start with the dog that requires a longer bath (the larger dog, the dog with more hair, etc.) and groom him first. After towel-drying the first dog, let him out of the room to run around and dry himself some more. Then bathe the second dog. When the second dog is finished with his bath and towel-drying, the first dog will be ready for his finishing touches.

6 · DO'S AND DON'TS

Do's

PREPARATION

1. Think of grooming as a pleasurable time with your best friend.
2. If you love grooming, so will your dog.
3. Remember that grooming is a way to keep your dog clean and healthy.
4. Go slowly at first, and you will build both your confidence and your dog's.
5. Be consistent about grooming.
6. Be sensitive to your dog's age whether he is four months old or fourteen years old.
7. Be careful on your older dog's back legs; they require gentle care.

BRUSHING

1. If your dog is not feeling well, you can lightly brush him primarily for the one-to-one attention it brings.
2. Always start brushing with your softest brush to make your dog feel relaxed.
3. When brushing your dog's face, keep the thumb and forefinger of your non-working hand outstretched just below the eye to protect the sensitive skin around the eyes.

4. Brush or comb your dog's hair on either side of his muzzle very gently and only for dogs with long hair on their faces.

5. When de-matting, always protect your dog by placing one hand tightly around the hair between the mat and skin.

NAILS

1. Hold your dog's paw in a straight line in back or in front, but never to the side.

EARS

1. Use a cotton ball with alcohol to clean your dog's ears. Massage the base of the ears gently as a reward after cleaning.

TEETH

1. Use a toothpaste for dogs or baking soda and water when brushing your dog's teeth.

BATH

1. Place a rubber mat in the tub or sink to prevent your dog from slipping.

2. Be very careful not to get water in your dog's eyes or ears.

3. Maintain a gentle but authoritative hand on your dog's back for support and reassurance.

4. Rinse completely and make sure all the shampoo and all the creme rinse is out after washing.

5. Make sure the area in which you are blow-drying your dog is totally dry.

Don'ts

PREPARATION

1. Do not seek perfection in grooming.

2. Never groom when you are rushed or feeling tired.

3. Don't get frustrated with a wiggly puppy. Give him time for a little puppy mischief.
4. Don't let one facet of grooming turn you off to the entire grooming experience.

BRUSHING

1. Do not brush sensitive areas of your dog.
2. Do not pull the skin underneath your dog's eyes while brushing or combing.
3. Never pull at a mat without protecting your dog.
4. Don't brush your dog's face if he doesn't need it.

NAILS

1. Never pull your dog's leg out to the side.

EARS

1. Never use a Q-tip or cotton swab in your dog's ears.

TEETH

1. Never use a toothpaste meant for people on your dog.

BATH

1. Never wash the insides of your dog's ears.
2. Don't run the air conditioner in the bath area.
3. Never leave glass bottles around the bathing area.
4. Never leave a dog unattended in the tub or sink or on any high place.
5. Don't call out, "Uh-oh" when it's time for the bath.
6. Don't let your dog go outside when he's wet unless it's warm.
7. Never bathe your dog if he is feeling ill or is on medication.

8. Never leave shampoo or creme rinse in your dog's hair. Rinse thoroughly.

9. Never use the blow-dryer on a hot heat setting. Unplug it when not in use.

10. Never point the blow-dryer at your dog's eyes, ears, or face.

APPENDIX: WHERE TO BUY SUPPLIES

The following is a list of distributors who sell to the general public. All of the catalogs are free except for J-B Wholesale Pet Supplies. I suggest getting a couple of catalogs to see which distributor accommodates you best. (Omaha Vaccine and Upco also carry veterinary supplies that are only available to veterinarians.) You may also find your local pet supply store a great resource for hard-to-find items. In New York City, I have found Paw 'N' Claw (543 LaGuardia Place, New York, NY 10012; 212-260-1767) a great place for ordering unusual or specialty items. Talk with the people at your favorite local store to see if they will order a special comb or shampoo that they don't usually have in stock.

The following catalogs offer all of the supplies mentioned in this book at very reasonable prices:

CHERRYBROOK
Route 57
Box 15
Broadway, NJ 08808
800-524-0820
In NJ: 201-689-7979

OMAHA VACCINE
3030 "L" St.
P.O. Box 7228
Omaha, NE 68107-0228
402-731-9600

DOGROOM PRODUCTS
544 Hempstead Ave.
West Hempstead, NY 11552
800-443-PETS
In NY: 516-483-8930

J-B WHOLESALE PET
SUPPLIES, INC.
22-02 Raphael St.
Fairlawn, NJ 07410
800-526-0388
In NJ: 201-791-1123

R. C. STEELE
15 Turner Dr.
Spencerport, NY 14559
800-872-3773
In NY: 716-352-3230

UPCO
3705 Pear
P.O. Box 969
St. Joseph, MO 64502
816-233-8800

ACKNOWLEDGMENTS

A special thank you to Alexander Yorinks, Lewis Jackson, Juliet Glass, Alexandra Chaprin, Mary Iucopilla, Richard Egielski, Denise Saldutti, Karen Etcoff, and Jeri Schatz. Thanks also to Janis Leventhal for allowing us to photograph her dogs for the cover of this book.

FREE! or under $1

—more than 200 toys and treats you can order by mail for your cat, listed in one handy new book!

Produced by Bruce Nash and Allan Zullo. Compiled by Maria E. Grau Dieckmann and Ginger Kuh. Illustrated by Mack McKenzie.

Only $4.95, **now at your bookstore,** or use coupon to order. **A PRINCE PAPERBACK**

CROWN PUBLISHERS, Inc., Dept. 983
34 Engelhard Ave., Avenel, N.J. 07001

Please send me FREEBIES FOR CAT LOVERS. I enclose my check or money order for $4.95 plus $1.00 postage and handling. 10-day money-back guarantee.

Name _____

Address _____

City _____ State _____ Zip _____

N.Y. and N.J. residents, add sales tax.